Greetings from
SAVANNAH
BEACH
Georgia

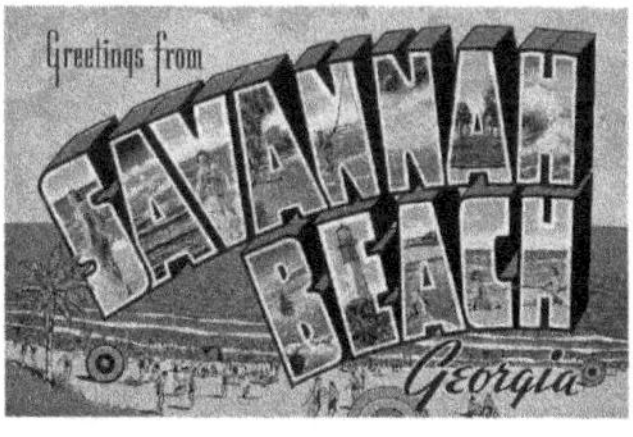
Greetings from
SAVANNAH
BEACH
Georgia

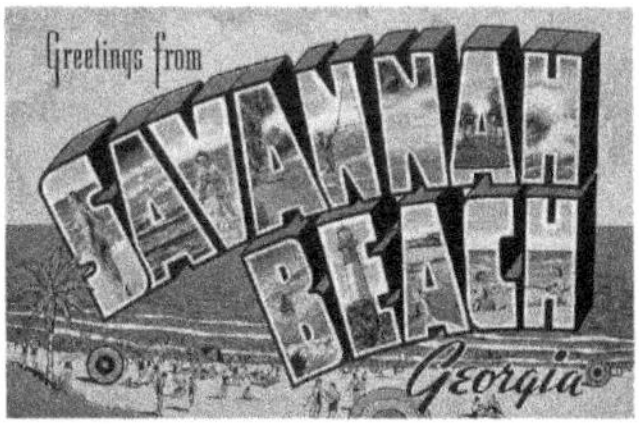
Greetings from
SAVANNAH
BEACH
Georgia

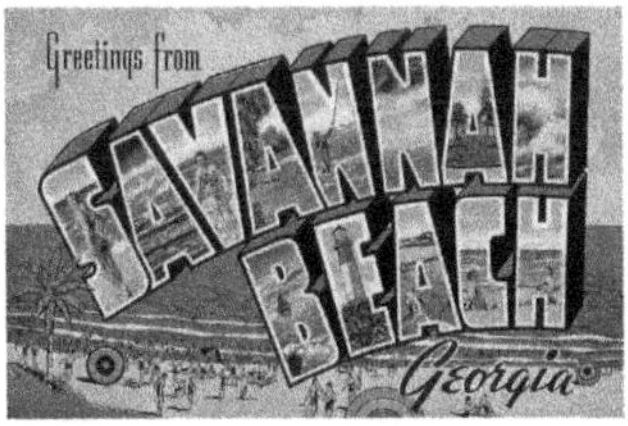
Greetings from
SAVANNAH
BEACH
Georgia

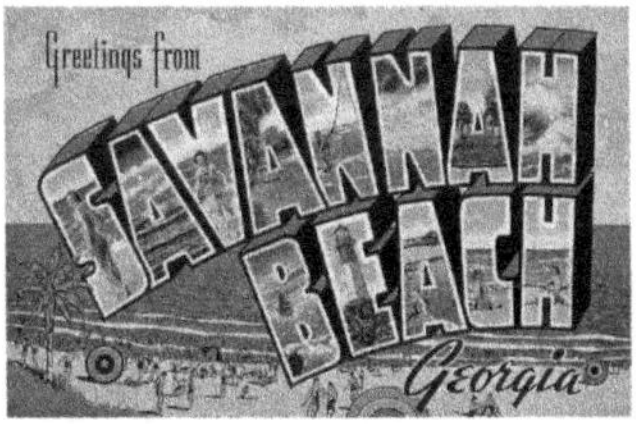
Greetings from
SAVANNAH
BEACH
Georgia

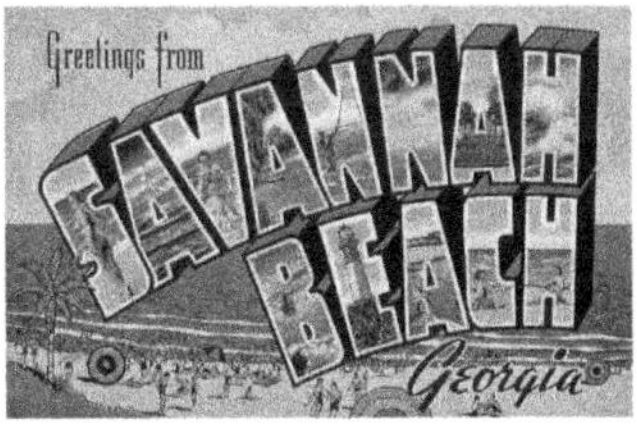
Greetings from
SAVANNAH
BEACH
Georgia

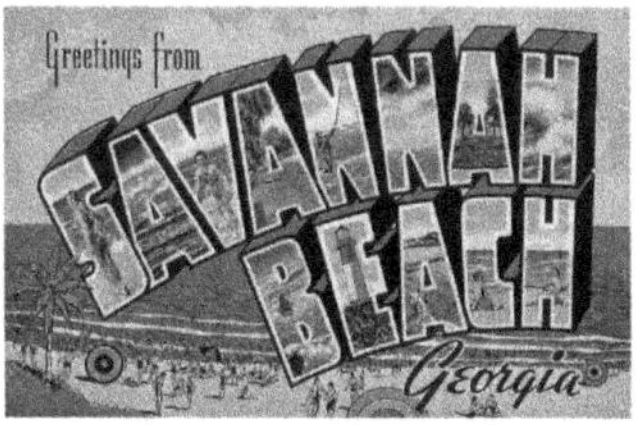
Greetings from
SAVANNAH
BEACH
Georgia

Greetings from
SAVANNAH
BEACH
Georgia

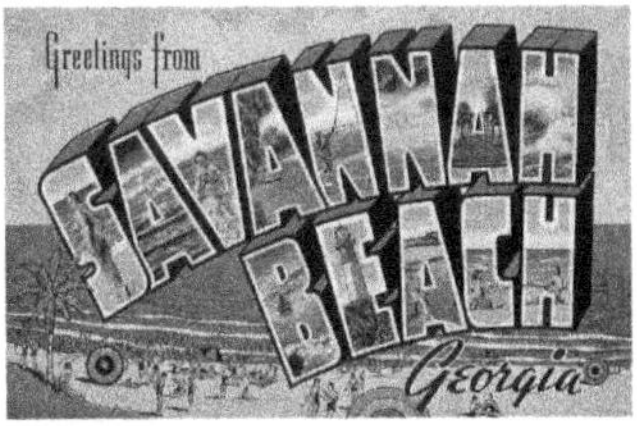
Greetings from
SAVANNAH
BEACH
Georgia

Greetings from
SAVANNAH
BEACH
Georgia

Greetings from
SAVANNAH
BEACH
Georgia

Greetings from
SAVANNAH
BEACH
Georgia

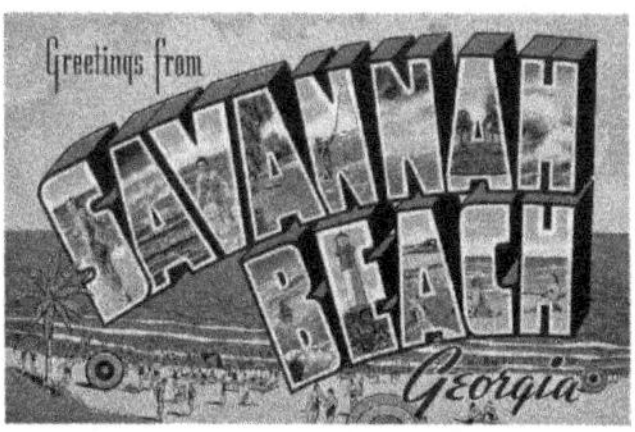
Greetings from
SAVANNAH
BEACH
Georgia

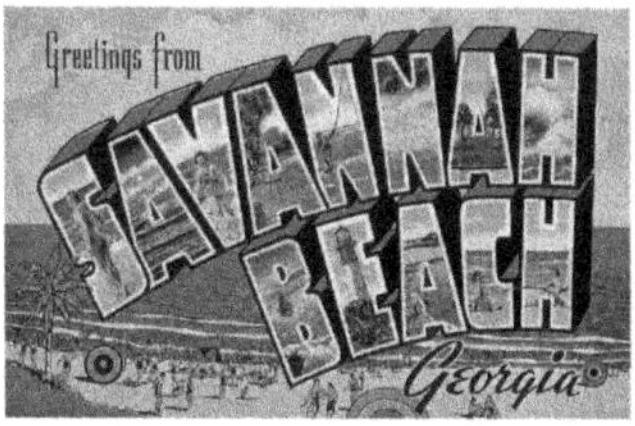
Greetings from
SAVANNAH BEACH
Georgia

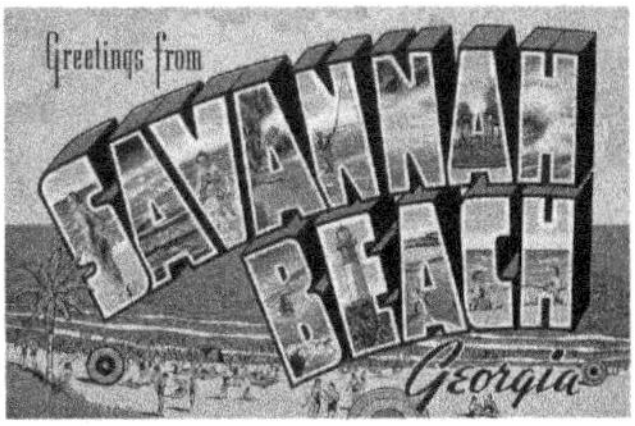
Greetings from
SAVANNAH
BEACH
Georgia

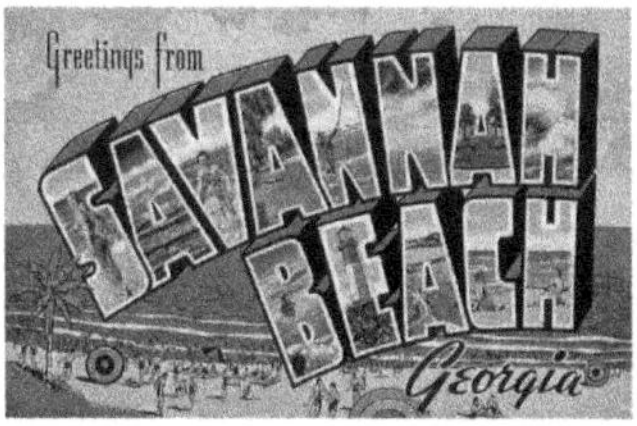
Greetings from
SAVANNAH
BEACH
Georgia

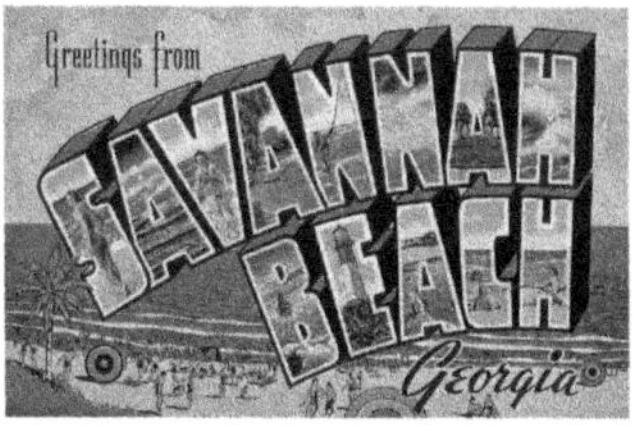
Greetings from
SAVANNAH
BEACH
Georgia

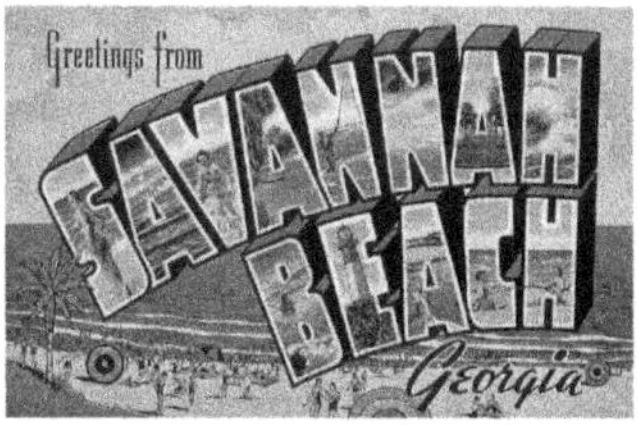
Greetings from
SAVANNAH
BEACH
Georgia

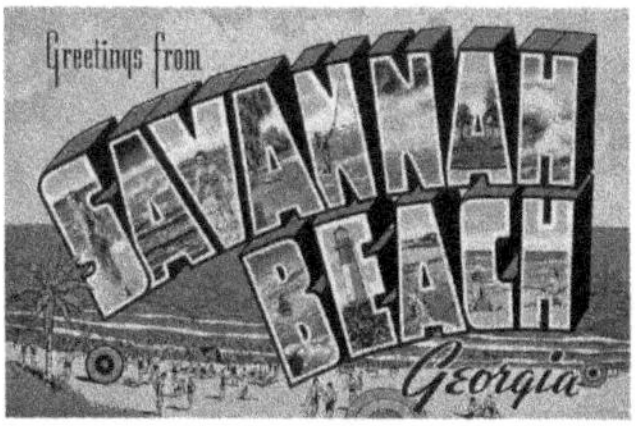
Greetings from
SAVANNAH BEACH
Georgia

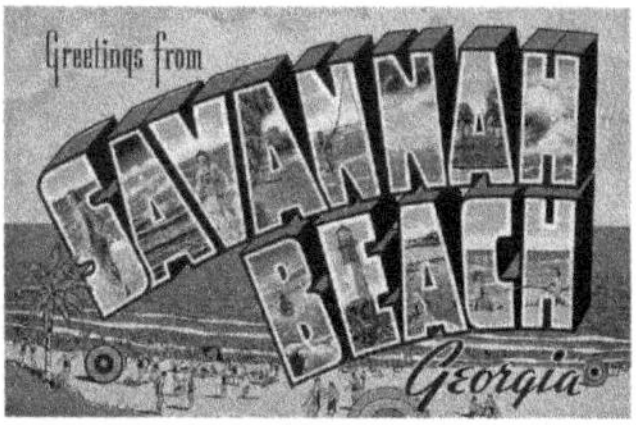
Greetings from
SAVANNAH
BEACH
Georgia

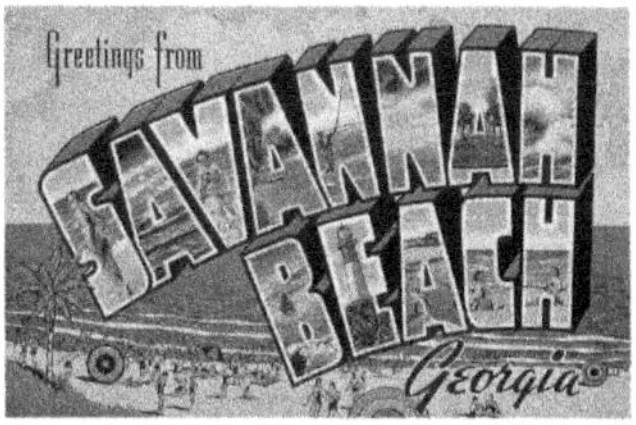
Greetings from
SAVANNAH
BEACH
Georgia

Greetings from
SAVANNAH
BEACH
Georgia

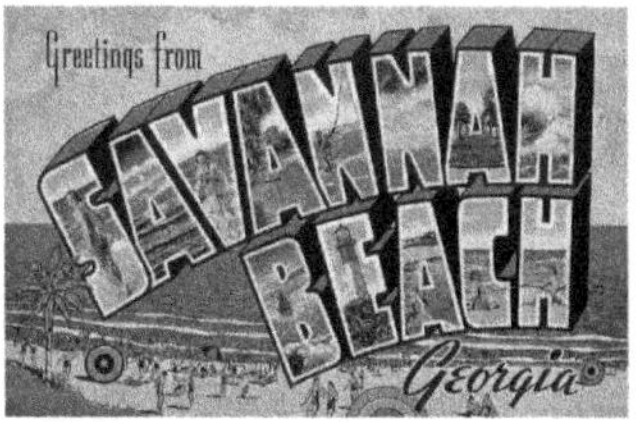
Greetings from
SAVANNAH
BEACH
Georgia

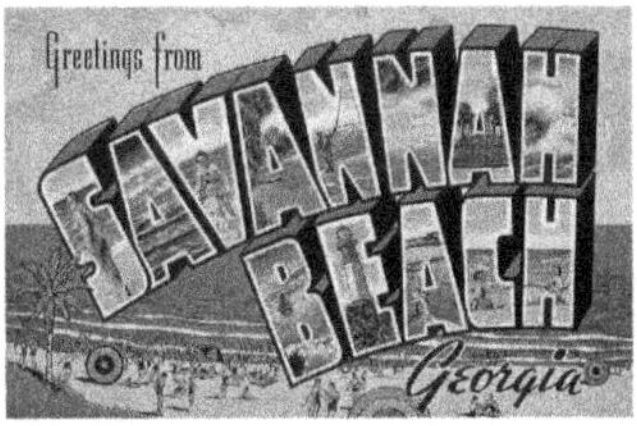
Greetings from
SAVANNAH
BEACH
Georgia

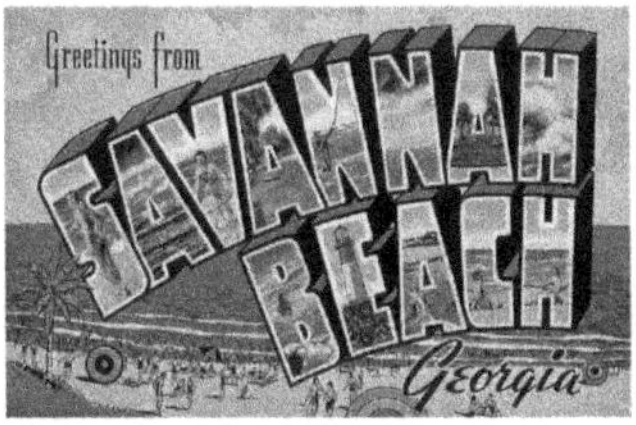
Greetings from
SAVANNAH
BEACH
Georgia

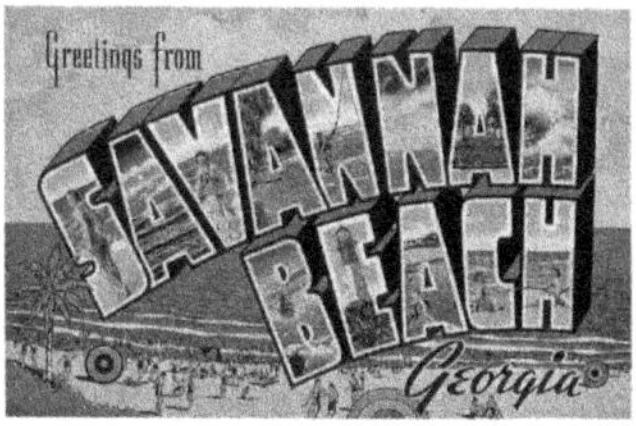
Greetings from
SAVANNAH
BEACH
Georgia

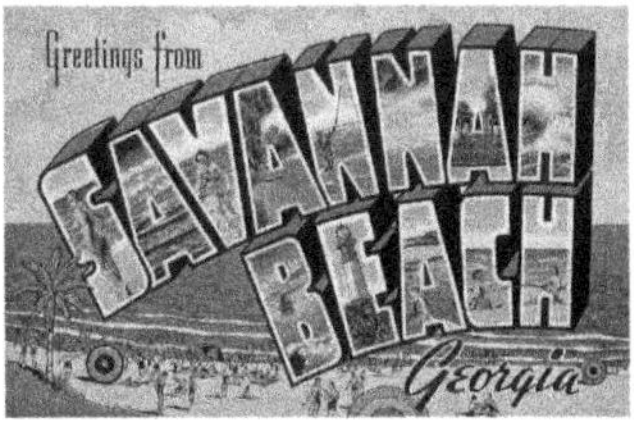
Greetings from
SAVANNAH
BEACH
Georgia

Greetings from
SAVANNAH
BEACH
Georgia

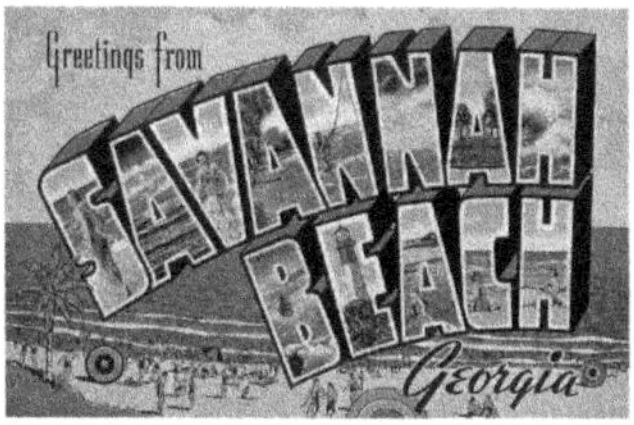
Greetings from
SAVANNAH
BEACH
Georgia

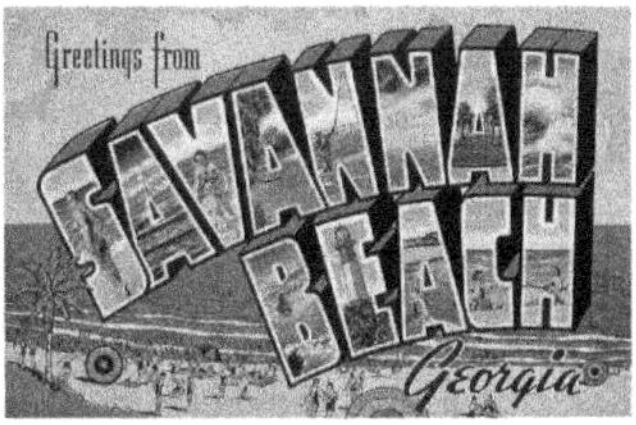
Greetings from
SAVANNAH
BEACH
Georgia

Greetings from
SAVANNAH
BEACH
Georgia

Greetings from
SAVANNAH
BEACH
Georgia

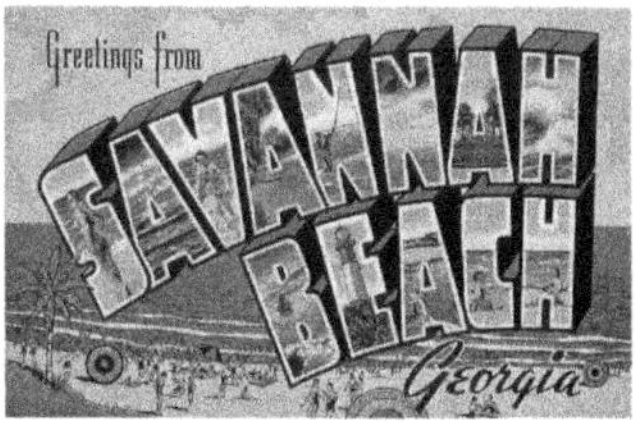
Greetings from
SAVANNAH
BEACH
Georgia

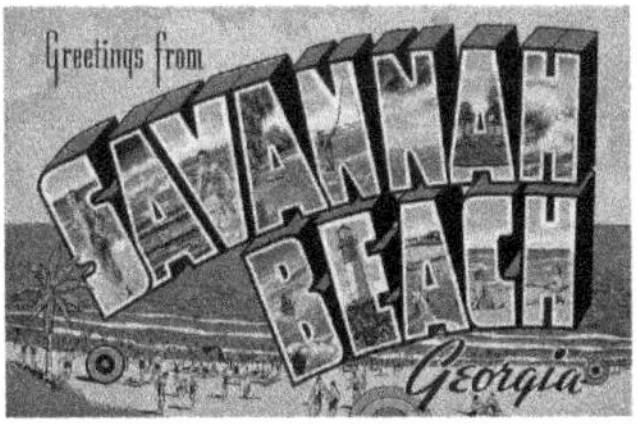
Greetings from
SAVANNAH
BEACH
Georgia

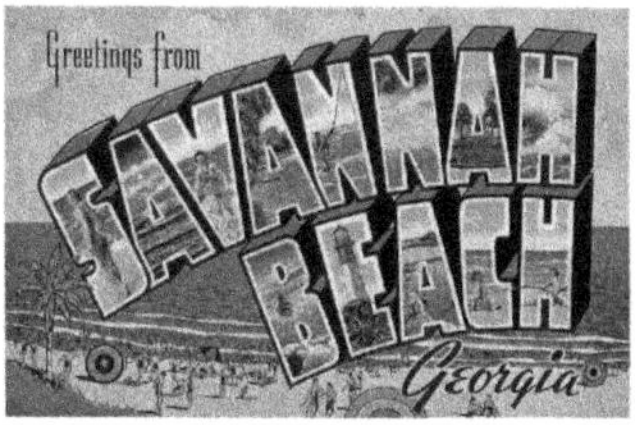
Greetings from
SAVANNAH
BEACH
Georgia

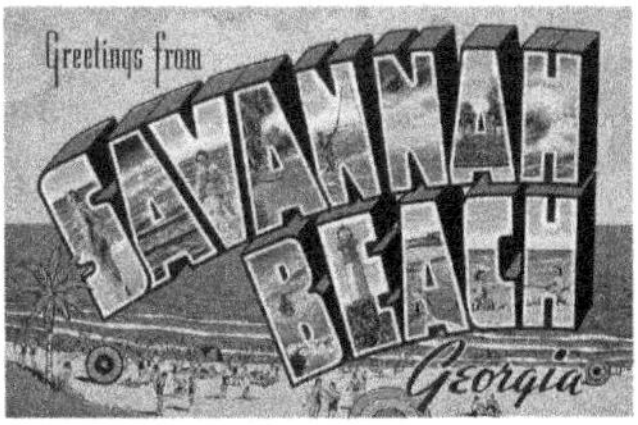
Greetings from
SAVANNAH
BEACH
Georgia

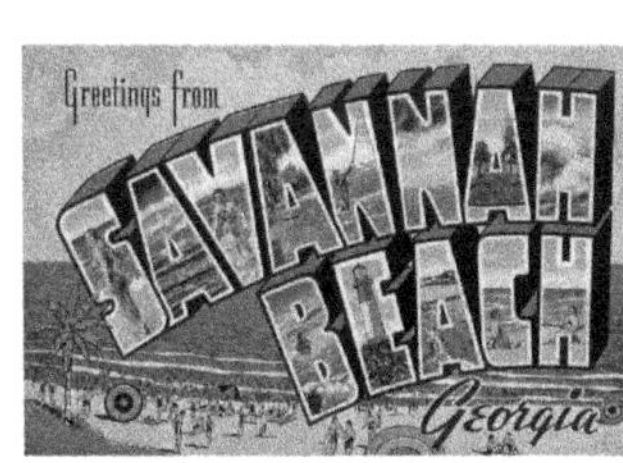
Greetings from
SAVANNAH
BEACH
Georgia

Greetings from
SAVANNAH
BEACH
Georgia

Greetings from
SAVANNAH
BEACH
Georgia

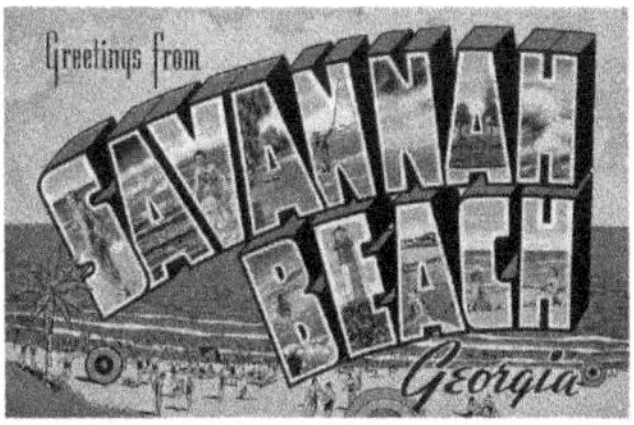
Greetings from
SAVANNAH
BEACH
Georgia

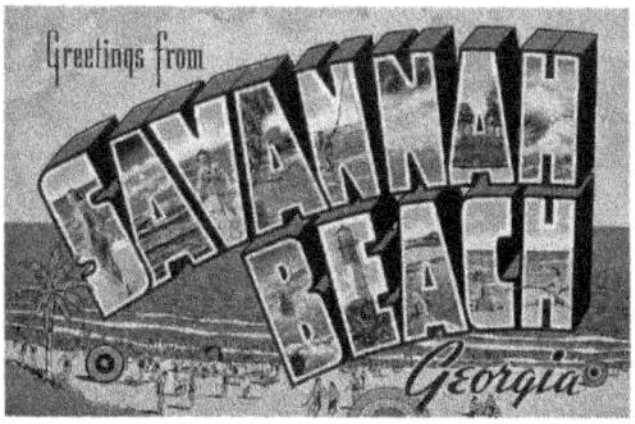
Greetings from
SAVANNAH
BEACH
Georgia

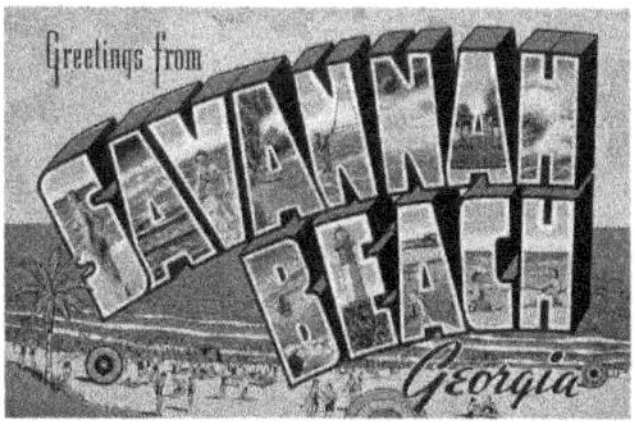
Greetings from
SAVANNAH
BEACH
Georgia

Greetings from
SAVANNAH
BEACH
Georgia

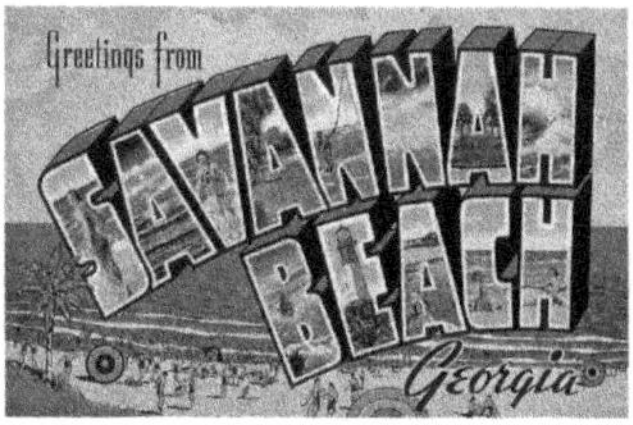
Greetings from
SAVANNAH
BEACH
Georgia

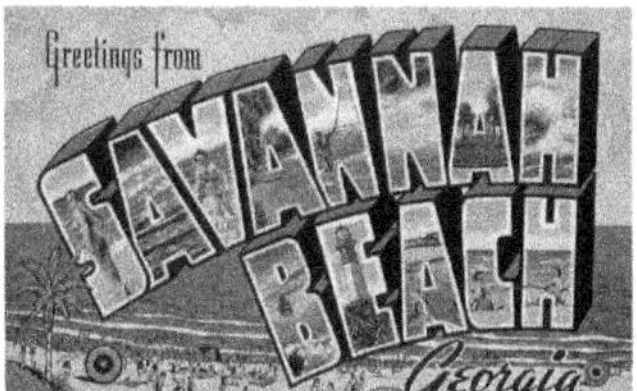
Greetings from
SAVANNAH
BEACH
Georgia

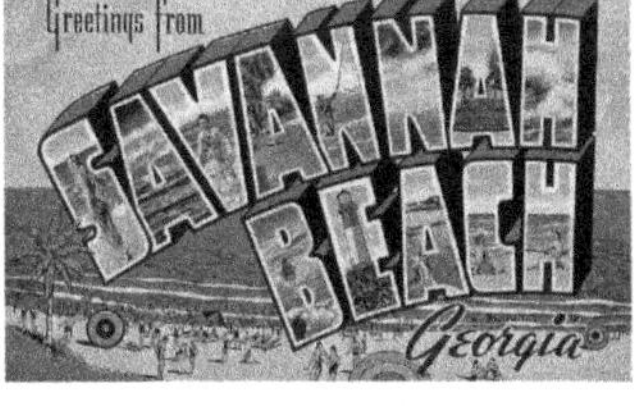
Greetings from
SAVANNAH
BEACH
Georgia

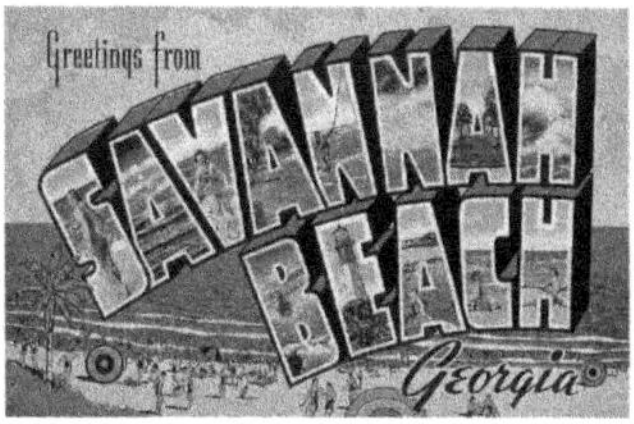
Greetings from
SAVANNAH
BEACH
Georgia

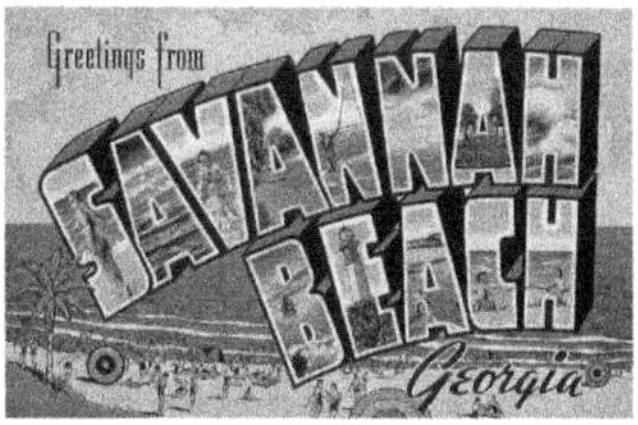
Greetings from
SAVANNAH
BEACH
Georgia

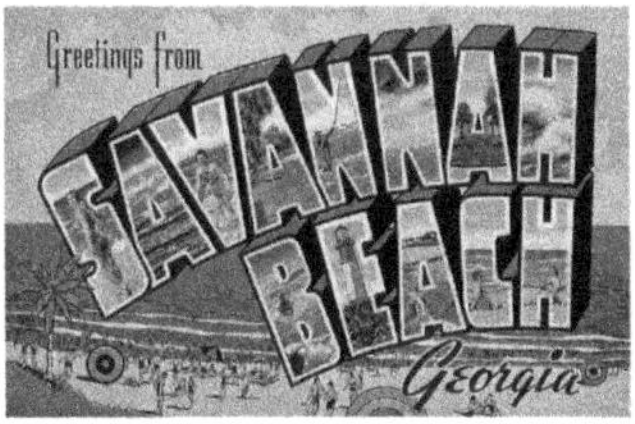
Greetings from
SAVANNAH
BEACH
Georgia

Greetings from
SAVANNAH
BEACH
Georgia

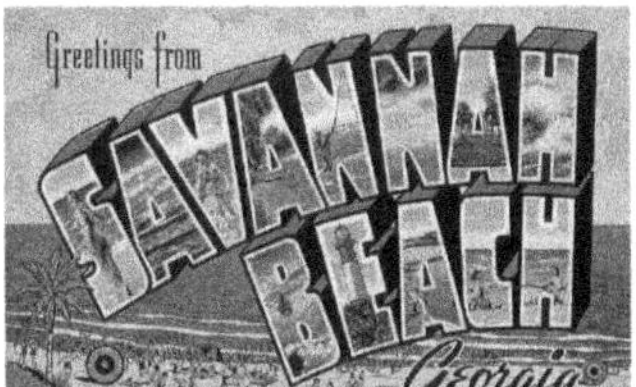
Greetings from
SAVANNAH
BEACH
Georgia

Greetings from
SAVANNAH
BEACH
Georgia

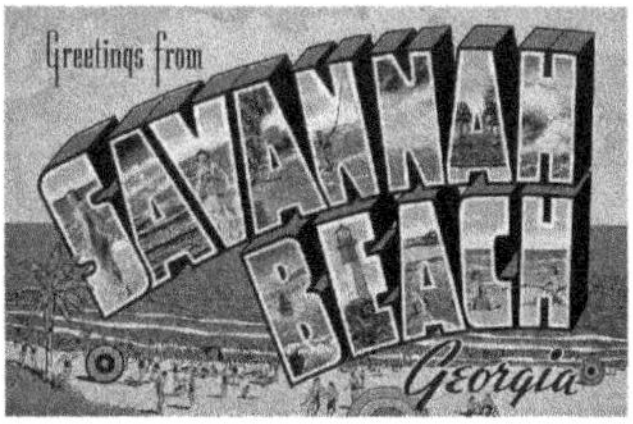
Greetings from
SAVANNAH
BEACH
Georgia

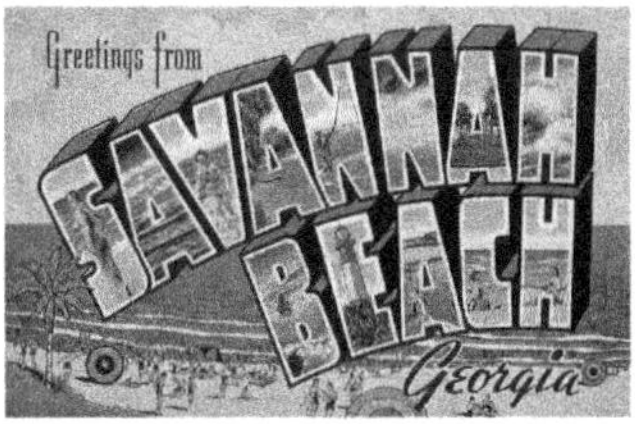
Greetings from
SAVANNAH
BEACH
Georgia

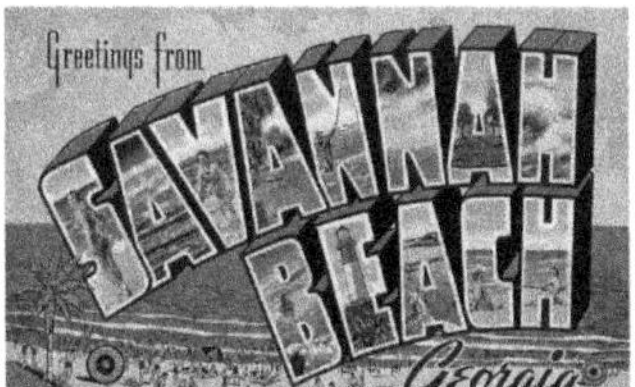
Greetings from
SAVANNAH
BEACH
Georgia

Greetings from
SAVANNAH
BEACH
Georgia

Greetings from
SAVANNAH
BEACH
Georgia

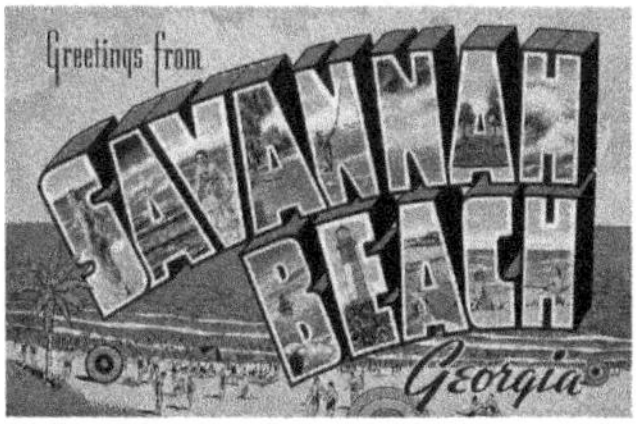
Greetings from
SAVANNAH
BEACH
Georgia

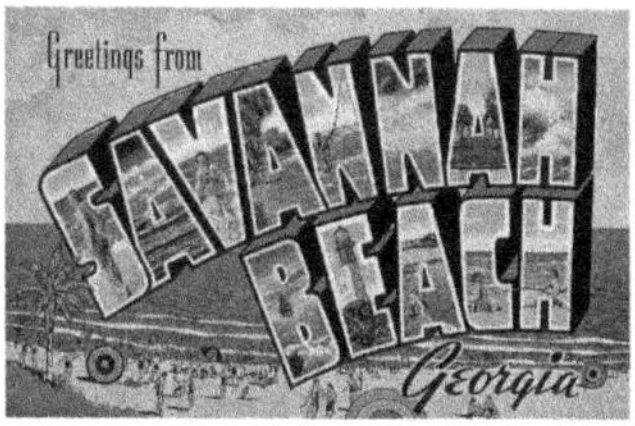
Greetings from
SAVANNAH
BEACH
Georgia

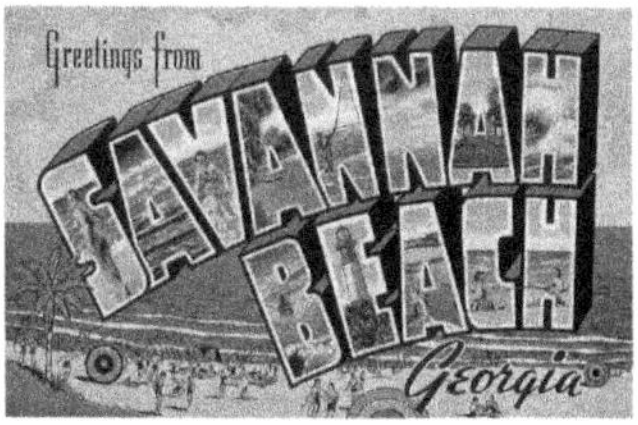
Greetings from
SAVANNAH
BEACH
Georgia

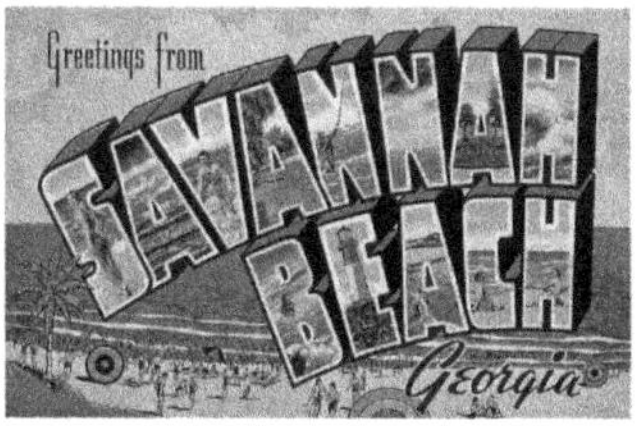
Greetings from
SAVANNAH
BEACH
Georgia

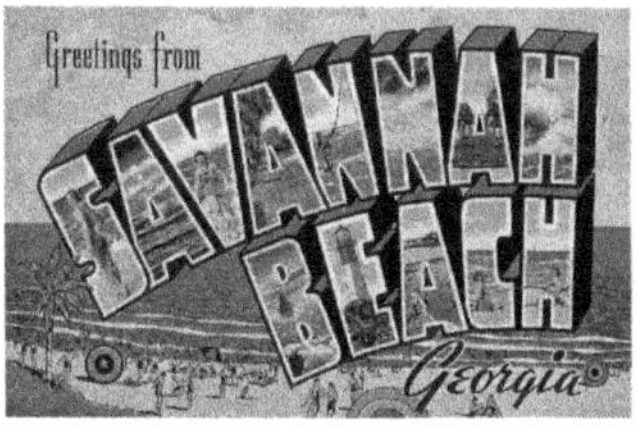
Greetings from
SAVANNAH
BEACH
Georgia

Greetings from
SAVANNAH
BEACH
Georgia

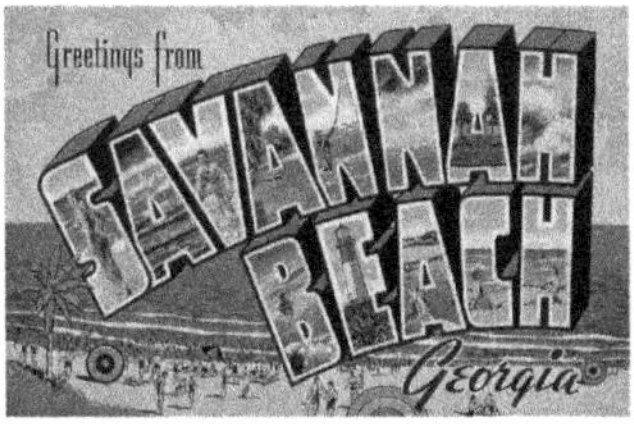
Greetings from
SAVANNAH
BEACH
Georgia

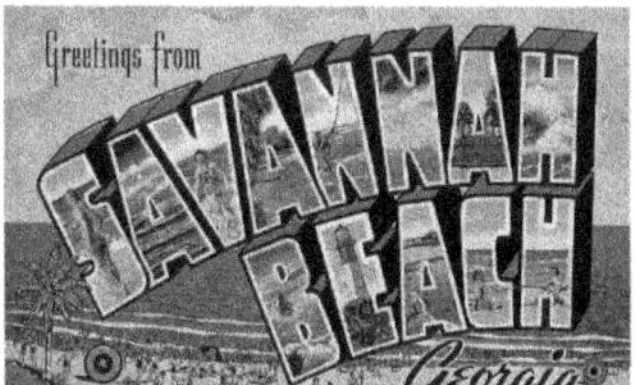
Greetings from
SAVANNAH
BEACH
Georgia

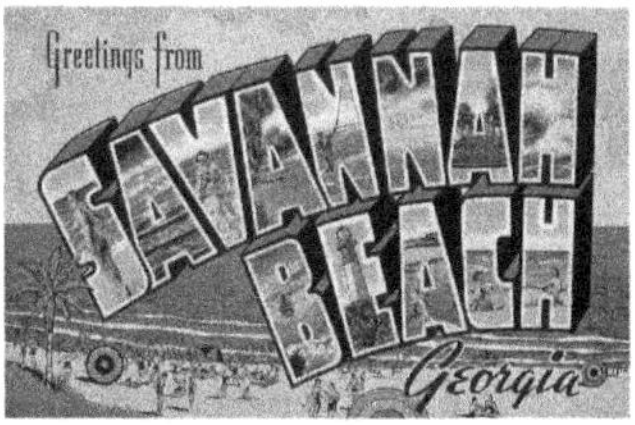
Greetings from
SAVANNAH
BEACH
Georgia

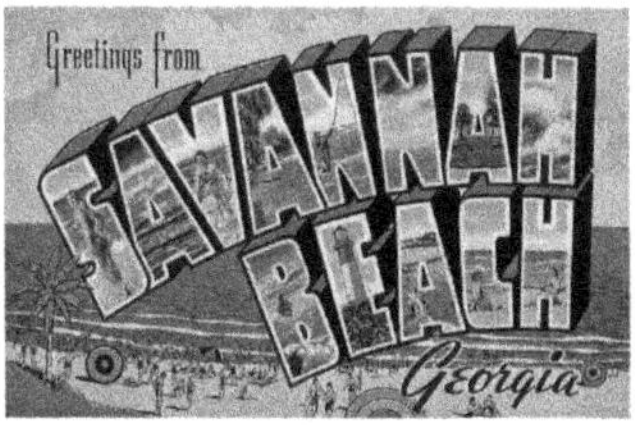

Greetings from
SAVANNAH
BEACH
Georgia

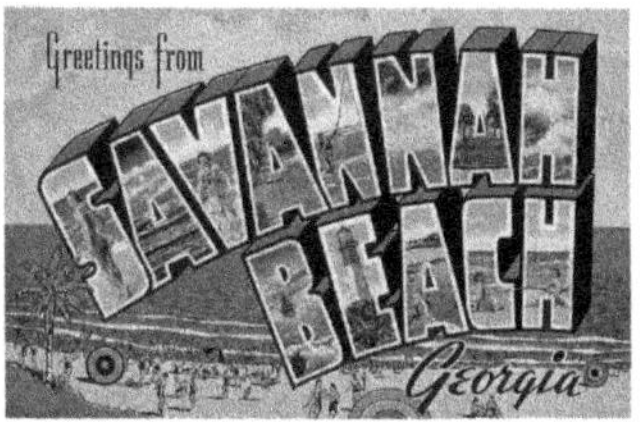
Greetings from
SAVANNAH
BEACH
Georgia

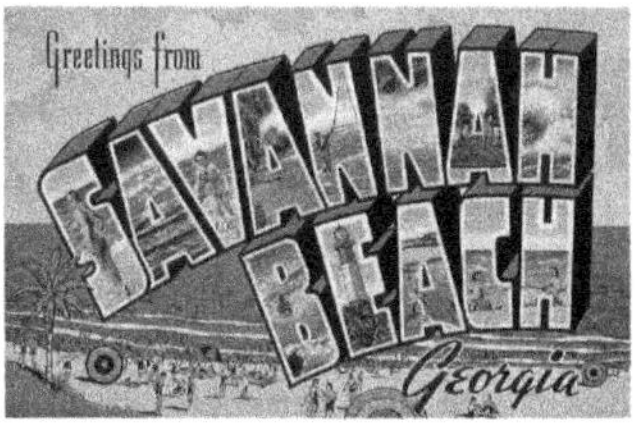
Greetings from
SAVANNAH
BEACH
Georgia

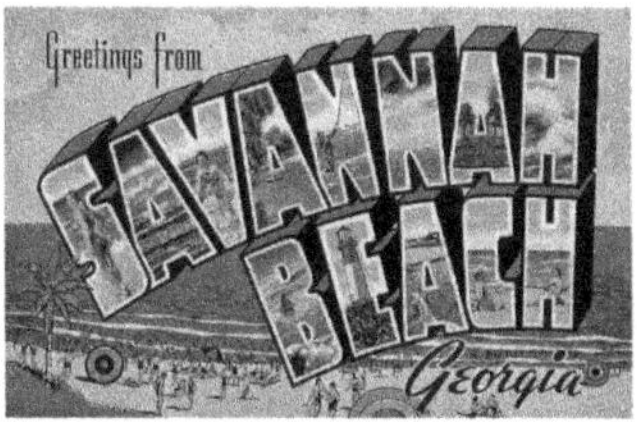
Greetings from
SAVANNAH
BEACH
Georgia

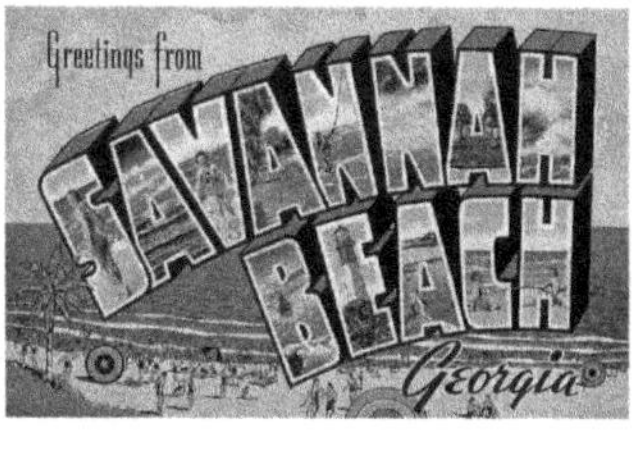
Greetings from
SAVANNAH
BEACH
Georgia

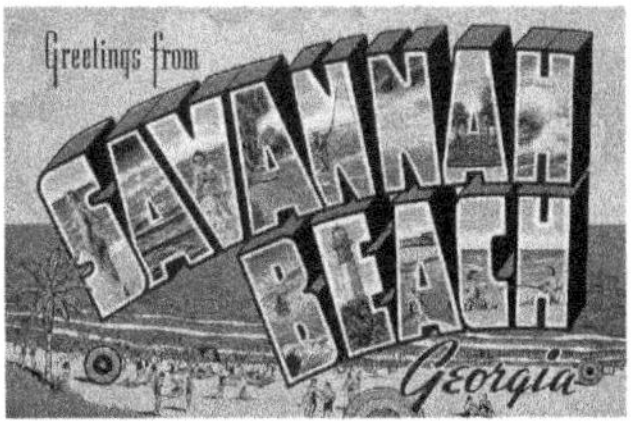
Greetings from
SAVANNAH
BEACH
Georgia

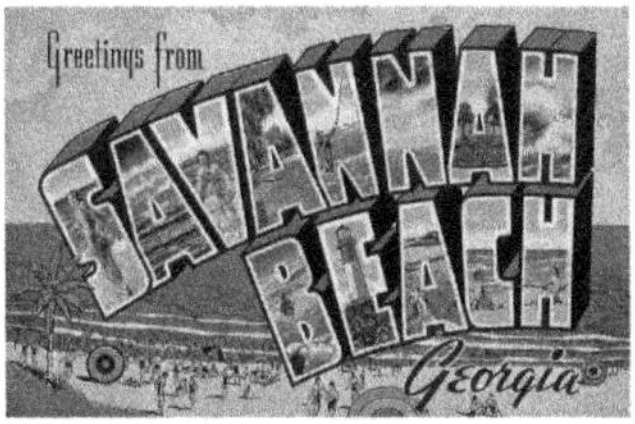
Greetings from
SAVANNAH
BEACH
Georgia

Greetings from
SAVANNAH
BEACH
Georgia

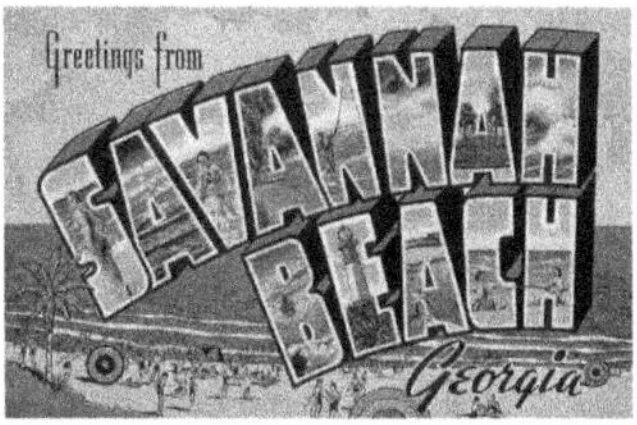
Greetings from
SAVANNAH
BEACH
Georgia

Printed in the USA
CPSIA information can be obtained
at www.ICGtesting.com
CBHW031315160724
11668CB00009B/368

9 798385 412419